How I Learned
To Learn New Things

poems by

Daniel Pereyra

Finishing Line Press
Georgetown, Kentucky

How I Learned
To Learn New Things

ACKNOWLEDGMENTS

Many of these poems first appeared, in some variation, in the chapbooks *Sunday Morning Ponderings* (Flutter Press, 2015), *Yes I Know You Can't Drive Across The World* (Red Bird Chapbooks, 2016) and *Just Another Love Poem* (Flutter Press, 2017). Others appeared in the following publications/sites: Red Fez (questions of purpose), Westward Quarterly (quiet observations), Poetry Quarterly (thinking in sunlight, some honesty on a tuesday), Third Wednesday (nightly conversations), and Avalon Literary Review (the sun is a yellow train in the sky). Immense thanks to the editors of these websites, journals and presses.

Publisher: Leah Maines

Editor: Christen Kincaid

Cover Art: Amos P. Schumacher "March"

Author Photo: Daniel Pereyra

Cover Design: Leah Huete

Printed in the USA on acid-free paper.
Order online: www.finishinglinepress.com
also available on amazon.com

Author inquiries and mail orders:
Finishing Line Press
P. O. Box 1626
Georgetown, Kentucky 40324
U. S. A.

Table of Contents

to gem & afp

questions of purpose

what is this thing
            —a poem—

that has no purpose
but to fill in the blank space
between each side
of this page

to show that indeed
i did think today

and ponder

and translate that mental
dance into
something concrete

                with which to remember
                the day

sunday morning pondering

i am wondering
who moved that chair to the space
just besides the door

where i will certainly trip
over it;

my knees finding
the one corner on the chair
that doesn't have cushion.

i am talented in that way—
that finds the hard points
in everything i walk by,

landing on my ass
with nary a lesson learned.

summer in the city

lazy fruit flies whisper secrets
to too hot fruit left on the counter.
the sun, she draws me out.

i wilt under her searching glare,
naked but for this sweat that
makes its way down my back.

fickle mistress touching each corner
of my second floor apartment
and yet i am drawn into her stare.

we burn

along a simmering city sidewalk
with a touch that never wavers,
and i'm left to wonder
how it was i fell for her again.

home

the sun dips lower than the
mountains let me see,
but i know she remains
despite my lack of sight.

purple clouds move through a lazy sky.

rain clouds threaten but
they lack conviction.

warm breezes move the air from
here to over the palms.

she hands me wine in a cup,
the rim stained red,
and lets me know the tomato plants
need more water.

new year

there beyond the double pane
of my kitchen window,
across a grass-stained yard—
lies a place to plant my tired feet.
plants reaching for the watering can
by the door.

and i am staring across the way
from my place by the sink;
soapy dishes clattering
from my fingers,
towards home.

constant questioning

i am trying to find a comfortable
spot

next to this cup of cold coffee.

      questioning the way
      it tastes like yesterday
      despite today's cream and sugar.

forced to live
in a world so consistently foreign,

trying to grab at the life
out in front of me,

              to pull
at the edges and fit inside.

mesquites in the yard

the mesquites in the yard cast
crooked shadows
over a wood slatted bench in the back,
with branches that look like
fingers reaching for my bare feet.
the grass (brown from the
late season) threatens to grab
hold of them, and so we
curl our toes to hide them away.
maybe we'll hang a tire
from the scraggly arms of the tree,
or plant an unassuming garden
to sit and watch as we drink our wine.
while a toddler swings,
legs kicking wildly in the air.

sometimes

i feel like a man without a country.
it happens when moving from one
place to another to find that the corners
are bodega-less.

so different, the streets no
longer match my footfalls.

i think of going home,
back to where the breezes
whisper my name
and sound like my mother
calling us in from the yard for dinner.

until, of course, i remember that i
am home.
and home has become a sun-kissed car,
old pennies lining the cup holders,
burning like bronze coals.

has become picking up my son and
making sure that his milk
is in the green sippy cup, not the
red sippy cup, which he swears
makes a difference.

home, where the barista at that one café
knows i'll have an iced coffee,
while sitting by the window where i can
look out into the street.

and every day is a homecoming
because i've made it so.

my life as the moon

bright against a studded sky,
i am the moon who brings up tides
in the wake of my rising.

half eye squinting between
ripened citrus trees. finite in my reach,

and yet

      far reaching,

stoic captain in a black sea.
yellow eyed demon & purveyor
of romantic and cursed alike
who howl for my favor
and sing to my good graces.

look at me, for i am the entryway
to a solitary chorus.
a portal through the thickness
of the dark.

the gilded silver of the nighttime sky,
eremitic and alone.

on movement and butterflies

we strike a conversation by the
lantanas,

        tiny blooms of yellow and red
        that ask to be held in a
        half-smile gaze,

and wonder on the best way
to get from flower
to
flower.

i suggest that she fly and
let the wind be her motor, or
anchor to her sail boat;

i've seen the
        way she moves, like

leaf
    and
        smoke.

she thinks i should take the bus,
(which when said out-loud is
of course absurd and shows
how little she's considered me.)

but maybe i'll walk instead
while she feigns envy at how
i strike out against the wind.

when really it is me who bleeds
with jealousy at the pace she keeps,
knowing i still have so much
yet to learn about flowers.

a discourse in self-awareness

there is this plant,
i think it may be a weed
but no one has told it,

reaching towards a laughing sun.
flat leaves dancing
in ambiguity.

it is living in my vegetable garden
between the tomatoes
and rosemary.

i feel like this weed—
an imposter. a conspirator

lying besides the long-limbed
flowering tomato plants
lining the flower bed.

autumn as a state of mind

ludicrous!
how fall winds feel like spring,
and plants call out to the november sun.
i am lost in the absurdity of yelling into an azure sky—
        "where is the real weather!"

i can hear the mocking bird songs;
chortles from grackles and summer sparrows,
and i am left alone
to wonder on the season.

ocean waves in amongst the oaks

how many times have i
felt

like the lone red
leaf lost within

the yellow and orange of
an autumn day.

branches bending reverently
in the wind,

lost in seasons,

on a rolling sea
of wind through trees.

      the sound of the serf;

ocean waves in amongst
the oaks and
fall hues.

the garden

a pineapple plant sticks out
its tongue from under
the window

daring me to believe
it is spring
and that pineapples will grow

in the desert.
dried up sage plants talk
amongst themselves,

planning a mutiny if they
don't get more cover.
(pineapple sage i think)

and they conspire against me
meeting with sagging tomatoes
to discuss the state of it all.

they wait for the mint,
who is bringing refreshments,
but are always late.

arriving with the
succulents from the other
side of the bricked walkway.

i'll hear them until late
in the night,
the strawberries always

talking out of turn.
and in the center of the fray,
is that damn pineapple top

who's yet to lay roots
there, beneath
the open window.

bolts

lettuce bolts reign high in gardens,
bolts of green stemmed, leafy stalks.
reign green giants, bitter and triumphant!
high stemmed bitter tasting flowering plants,
in leafy and flowering majesty grow.
gardens, stalks; triumphant plants grow rebelliously.

a thought about the back yard

i only notice the beryl
shades in the otherwise dry grass.

places where the smell of fresh soil
is more than just the smell of dirt;

growing things coming from below,
if only I would take the time to notice

them break through the ground.
where the buds on an orange tree

get me giddy with anticipation
for the sweetness to come.

dirt in my water and other musings

there is dirt in my water,
flecks of granular nothings
swimming in my liquid respite.
here where the blue sky meets the

heat dancing away from
an indifferent sun. and a toddler
dances to the sounds of
dry leaves, themselves dancing

to an orchestra of wind in the trees.
chalk mixes with the sweat on my palms.
i am partial to green,
(how it colors my calloused fingers.)

water-stains mar the pebbled deck,
complete with a wooden table upended
by tiny hands and rolling along
its squared edges.
                    .
i point to a sparrow sitting next
to another on a tree branch.
          "we know the sounds a bird makes."
my arms are out stretched

like wings. he nods.
          "and what sound does a monkey make?"
he asks.
          "ooh ooh ooh."

raining in the desert

rain is falling in the desert.
not a metaphor but what i see
looking out of my bedroom window.

      & the ground is not
      ready for all this rain.

so tiny rivers run in every direction
and form a tiny pond
that soon becomes a tiny lake.

      because the ground just can't
      handle all this rain.

so the tiny lake becomes
a tiny ocean for the ants
to worry over,

and this is what happens
when it rains in the desert.

una observación desde el patio

la luz toca mi cara
tan fuerte, yo parpadeo.

cubriendo con mi mano lo
que hace que las plantas crescan.

lo que crea la vida
bloqueado por mis pequeñas manos,
con un suciedad
todavia abrazando mis palmas
          desde trabajar en el jardín.

mis manos
deben tener un poder
desconocido
para parar el sol de brillar.

*****

the light touches my face
so strongly that i blink.

covering with my hands,
that which makes the plants grow.

the creator of life
blocked by my small hands,
with dirt
still hugging my palms
          from working in the garden.

my hands
must have a power,
hidden,
to stop the sun from shining.

cafe

i

this coffee
black but for the
two creamers
   (hazelnut)

sears my tongue
so that i will be reminded
   of its sweet and bitter
   bite for hours

yet i can't seem to
wait to take another sip

   and let it burn
   me again

wake me—
so that i close my eyes
   from the heat of it

ii

i am reminded of drinking
too-strong coffee made in
a heaving iron percolator
that lived on my mother's stove

i can still hear the water rising in fits
through coarsely ground beans

we drank the coffee
with buttered toast
cut in half and spilling crumbs
onto the floral table cloth
the bread dipped in the inky sweetness

steaming in an old mother's day mug

iii

i will be the first to admit—
      we drink day old coffee

in fact we make too
much at a time

      so that on those off-center mornings
we just heat it up

      —add some warm milk,
      two teaspoons of sugar

and savor the mature flavor
while watching a toddler
eat his cereal.

      see my face /
      it is shameless and guilt free

quiet observations

the plants need more watering—
their light green turning
to dusk-like shades.

      dust collects
      on wrinkled book covers
          dog-eared / coffee-stained
      from bouts with sunday mornings.

curtains dance on frayed legs
to the tune of a warm breeze
coming from the window.

but my eyes remain
      focused
on my son's rising chest,
a devious smile as he sleeps.

      and at once the plants are greener
      the breeze brings scents
      of street life,

and the books—worn and
used as they are—
become more new.

another song to dance to

spring rains linger
on the dry grass.

my feet are wet.

the flowers enjoy an
unscheduled drink,
shaking green fists at the sun,

and we stomp around the
yard so that mud sticks to
our soles.

      you see,
      when it rains in the desert
      the vegetables sing!

and me without my shoes,
i can't help but
dance in step to the tune.

rain on a friday afternoon

i am standing in a summer rain
storm, feet planted firmly
in a puddle that feels like a warm bath,

because this is what it means to get
rain in the desert.

the kind that washes away the heat,
and lingers like camp-fire smoke
in my clothes.

that sounds like a child's recital, drops
ringing off of mint leaves,
or drumming in an empty tin can that
might finally be allowed to rust.

and even though the concrete is
already drying, the moisture jumping
into the air as if it were walking barefoot
on a summer day,
the air will still smell like mowed
grass.

the parking lot by
frys will still be flooded;
a lone shopping cart left swimming in the
tepid water

a saturday morning

there is a cold breeze coming
from the crack in the window
over my bed.

it cools the skin
peeking from out fleece blankets.

all i want is to drink the coffee waiting
for me in the coffee pot in the kitchen,
prepared the night before,

only, i have to get up and get it.
a gray cat whispers in my ear.
an orange cat sits at my feet.

we stare at the ceiling,
at the birds flying by outside.

we play tug-o-war with the sheets
and i tell anyone who'll listen
that i just want coffee,
and the damn window fixed.

monday afternoon

i am caught in a doldrum;
a single, solitary something
you can catch with two hands,
lift high above your head
and hold in the rain
outside a stranger's apartment.

caught, wishing i could just let it go
back into the heavens
where doldrums live along side
a young man's regrets.
drinking cheap wine with pinkies
raised high.

and i am caught!
eyes cast towards tuesday.

some honesty on a tuesday

there is that time in the morning—

when bird songs mingle with the
sound of the sprinklers coming alive.

the gurgling of a percolator floats
through the still air,

and the sun breaks through the distant
haze, scaling single story houses
like an olympic hurdler.

—that i think with sincere clarity,
drinking my coffee with eyes closed:

damn, i'm tired.

nightly conversations

we have the same conversation each night,
a debate on which blanket to use
and whether the ceiling fan
is turned on too high, or
if the air conditioner is set to
the correct temperature.
did i remembered to lock all the doors?
did we feed the cats and change their water,
and do we have any water, which means
that i have to get up now and get her some.
but then we remember that i locked all the doors
in between commercial breaks,
and the cats will end up drinking the water
left by the side of the bed.
she throws off the blankets in the middle of
the night anyway,
and i always adjust the thermostat
at two in the morning
on my way back from the kitchen.

you can't tell me about true love

i read a poem about true love once,
with idyllic images of lilies
and sunbeams and other nonsense
that some poet probably made up
while sitting in his long johns.
which coincidently is what true love
really looks like:
like 2am conversations about what picture
to hang in the living room or
keeping quiet when you reach
for the last piece of red velvet cake,
because i know it is your favorite
and we'll work if off during our evening walk.
it is carrying a tricycle three
blocks in the crook of my arm even though
our son swore he would ride it,
& instead now hangs precariously
from your shoulders.
and i have never seen cherubs with bows
or strolled through a pastoral field,
but i have shared a sink while brushing my teeth
and carried your coffee to the car when
your hands were full.
have held your tired head in my lap,
finger pressing the spot between your eyes
while you sleep.
and you can't tell me that isn't
what true love looks like.

summer from a red tub

the hose sprays into the air with
mini rainbows

flashing inside
long arcs of water.

my son yells "i'm wet!",
and i offer him the blue towel

though we both know he doesn't really
want to get out of this makeshift pool;

       a red plastic tub he can only *just*
       fit his body into.

enough to keep him busy for twenty
minutes

while i sit nearby,
sweat pooling in the crook of my elbow,

fanning myself with the book of
poems i thought i'd read.

but i've just been too busy
watching the poetry of him splash at the bees,

stick-legs dangling
over the plastic sides

while his toes drip onto the
dry grass.

in the desert,
summer comes in may,

happy to settle over a lazy sunday afternoon

and into a red plastic tub

full of cold hose water,
and i feel like i could live in this

moment forever,
or at least until the sun goes down.

his eyes help me remember

something in my son's
wild-eyed expressions, help me remember

watching my dad mow the lawn;
baseball playing
on a grass stained am/fm radio
and a sweat dampened shirt

hanging from his slight frame.
watching him with a rake in my
hand and a scowl on my face.

> slapping at the mosquitoes
> making a picnic lunch of my ankles.

i raked grass clippings, snaking them into large
black garbage bags,
leaving the backyard looking like we did after
one of his basement haircuts.

and when we'd go back inside,
my mother waited

with a glass of cool water and
boiled plantains, mashed
with fried eggs and canned fish.

ending the night with his famous papaya shake,
tasting like childhood in a metal cup.

afternoons in the backyard

there is no question that
i can feel complete
waist-deep in an orange kiddie pool,

waves made by a toddler's splashing.
in those shallow depths, i am a hero.

a fighter of bees and tantrums alike
with only the afternoon sun as my shield
& imagination my sword.

or trident, in keeping with
the theme.

and the sharks!

the kind that attack from behind
inflatable plastic balls.

and together we vanquish
them all before being called inside
for dinner.

a lesson from the piano man

it's just a coincidence that i am listening
to billy joel, while sitting in a
hot car on the way to pick up my son.

re-living a life i never lived, while
driving with the top down in a car
i never owned.

and feeling like i won't ever have
to go back /

to where? i couldn't tell you,
but i'm here now and billy is telling me
this is my life

and i believe him. each and
every piano key, i believe him.

i'm driving, but not towards mac'n'cheese
dinners and an 8pm bedtime,
but towards a life too loud for these quiet
neighborhood roads.

a life i never lived but am living now
while billy sings and tells me
that this is **my** life, so leave me alone.

> until, of course it's not my life
> because now it's *his* life
> and that's ok.

he tells me about his day and
how he likes mac'n'cheese dinners
& 8pm bedtimes and
pulling on the cat's tail just to see him run.

> that's ok with me billy,
> because like you said, this is my life.

the sun is a yellow train in the sky

i live for car-ride conversations
about his day,
where he tells me he drank
milk and played on the swings,

that the wheels
on the city bus go round and round,

and he wants to eat candy
for dinner and watch that one show
about trains and speaking of:

> did i know that
> the sun is a yellow train in the sky?

he tells me that the car next to us
is driving too fast so i should be careful,
which i assure him i am.

he waves to the passerby's and yells
"hello!" at the top of his lungs. and now
he's made friends with half of the city.

and when we get home he takes the
keys from my hands and opens the door
announcing to the cat lounging on
the kitchen table that he has come home.

the yellow swing

there / beneath
the yellow swing

and my son's dangling
feet,

i see the future in the
space between

the plastic and the high grass
& can't help

a thankful smile.

small journeys

i aspire to write poetry that is grand,
the kind that sweeps from bleak
to cheerful in under twenty lines.

        something profound like keats,
        whitman or seuss.

yet when i sit at my desk, typing with only
four of my fingers,

and the cats outside wrestle with sunflowers,
or grackles swooping at the stale
bread we left for them earlier that morning,

already i am miles from where i started,
with a coffee in my hand and
toddler on my lap, laughing at the
silly animals outside.

redecorating

there is a spider web resting
in the corner
where the flower pot
meets the wall of the house.

it is full of dry leaves
and purple flower petals.

i can't help but wonder
if the spider who made this was happy
with the decorating,

or like me, feels that it is
just good enough.

which is how i feel when looking
at the bare spaces on our walls,
knowing there is a box of
picture frames collecting dust
in the closet.

on the mysteries of attics

i was amazed to learn
that we have an attic,
and that this attic is already full
of someone else's nothings,
stored and forgotten
after a messy move perhaps.
so i wonder what my own mystery
attic might hold
if i were to throw away
the nothings i go through
on rainy afternoons, the ones
that prove i am living a full life,
and i wonder if this is a metaphor
for the places in my mind
where nothings go to die,
waiting for the next owner
to find between old crutches
and a box of discontinued
christmas ornaments.
but i'm not really one for metaphors.
just someplace to store
the old shelves i swear i'll
mount on the next
rainy afternoon.

creativity

creativity,
like a struck match,
burns for me
too quickly /

      bright
and fast,
leaving whispers
of sulfurous
smoke.

a process

submitting work
to be published,

      like stepping into a downpour,

is to submit yourself
to the elements
in a way not felt since
the first people leapt

across the high grassed plains
towards sustenance and survival,
away from the waiting
maws of a lion.

at the library

there is nothing running
through this
part of my brain,

the part i leave open
for running.

so imagine
my surprise at this
lack of

running.

just illegible words
strewn around a hand written
note book.

i am lost in the reference
section and asking for help,
wishing we were allowed to run,

so fast
the librarian could only offer

an angry glance instead
of pointing to the where i can find
the books on writing.

the fire-less heathen

torn matchbooks litter the ground.
my fingers burn from the friction
but i can't start a fire
no matter how hard i try.

sun-dried wood stands
like an alter
where offerings are left
to me, the fire-less heathen.

and taking the sticks of
phosphorus from my hands,
she stands with hair blowing
in a late fall breeze

like a missionary
come to show me the error of
my polytheistic ways.

      she ignites the wood with a single match
      the way a believer tries to ignite
      the soul of an infidel,

and i am in awe of her
magic, scared of what it will mean
when she later asks me to
put it out.

summer wine tasting with friends

there is a curious fly who
upon smelling the pinot
noir in my glass

wanted to know the year
the grapes had been
picked and if i planned

on drinking it with cheese
or with fresh fruit harvested
only that morning.

and i know this fly is curious
because it is still swimming in
my wine glass, making small

circles in the middle of
my evening drink; here
where even the flies fancy them-
selves wine connoisseurs.

i wouldn't say i'm lonely

i am not lonely *per se;*
not like the last slice of week-old
bread or the jelly bean forgotten
in the bag before throwing it away.

not the kind of lonely that
warrants a pat on the back,
cigarettes in the cold

and listening to classic rock while
            drinking the last beer in a six pack.

no, i am lonely
the way fish in a school are lonely.

how mountains are lonely,
with only birds and wind and rain and
the almighty himself for company.

lonely the way that first star peeking through
the clouds at night is lonely, or
how the moon rising full faced is lonely.

or how the earth is lonely
when she looks around the solar system
and only sees rocks.

it is a stone in my shoe

this thing—
i shake my foot
but i'm walking and i don't
stop walking
       so i hop.

can you see me
       hopping?

it makes for such a foolish
sight, and i know
i should stop and take off
my shoe.

turn it
       upside
             down,

let the stone roll out
onto more solid ground.
but you know how it is

when you've just been
       walking so long

the stone feels like a part
of your foot.

       such a part
       you forget how it feels
       without it.

because i only kind of remember
what it feels like
walking

on   air

instead of sore feet /

    hopping
simply because i like to hop.

a reminder

i've never really known tragedy;
one of those lucky few who've
stayed free from the types
of experiences that knuckle against
your forehead in a tightened fist.

not that i haven't tasted the bitterness
of remorse, or danced alone to the entropic
sounds of regret. Yet,

i *have* been relatively free
of tragedy.

and i remind myself of this
in those times i am feeling like
no one could have it worse than me,

simply because i burned my
tongue on tomato soup,
which always leads to bouts of
cheerlessness at the state
of things.

ok now i get it

summer days get to me,
those of triple digit temperatures
& sweat burning my eyes.
which leads me to wonder
how wars are fought
in the desert,
when all i want is
a cool drink and the air conditioning
cranked to antarctic levels.
but then i wonder, really, why
are *any* wars fought anymore
when it makes more sense
to settle all disputes
with a drawn out game of monopoly.
and homemade biscuits,
though if i'm honest
i wouldn't dream of turning
on the oven in this heat.
and no one can ever decide
who gets to be the little dog
or the racecar, though i for one
prefer the old shoe.
so, i guess that's why
we still fight wars.

yes i know you can't drive across the world

i find i make a lot of lists;
short lists and longer lists
of things i'd like to accomplish in
life or just get done this weekend

from finishing that one book,
to changing the light bulbs in the
pantry

and
sometimes it's bigger things like
making a chair

       because i really want
       to make a chair, from
       the mesquite branches i cut last week

sometimes it's even bigger
things, like living in a lake-side
town in guatemala

or buying a trailer and driving across
the world

then sometimes it gets too big,
like discovering a new element,
traveling back in time or building a spaceship

       out of the mesquite branches i cut
       last week

assuming i have enough wood left
after making the chair

first meetings

i didn't notice you there,
smiling a brooklyn sunshine
over park slope smile.

but you saw me,
hands still clammy
in black knit gloves.

we ate fish tacos,
and drank cheap beer while our
knees touched.

and when we left to go
our separate ways,
you turned back as if to say to me

from half way down the block,

"come back and
kiss me you idiot!"

what it is i think i know

i think i know what it is—
the love between two people.

know that loneliness
can be like the air
& love like water on parched lips,

and i know air and water
enough to drink between
the gasps of breath.

a bird and her muse

a bird perched on my shoulder,
small fluttering thing.
so light and full of color that
she blends into the summer sky.

you see, i am her perch—
the unmoving surface on which she stands;
blank canvas for her droppings.
a patchwork of colors on my arms.

i am her muse,

she sings to me, beats wings against
my cheek, and when she flies away
i watch for her return.

when we meet in the in-between

there is a silence that belongs to everyday.
the kind you bathe in or leave to rise like dough,
and i live in this silence.

the in-between spaces that never seem to fill in.

       i dance in this space!

to music made from the pauses between words,
and this is where she finds me;
across a busy street with a coffee in my hand.

her eyes tell me she's been there too,
that she is also swimming in the still waters
of silence and empty spaces.

our hands meet from across the road,
walking side by side from different
ends of the sidewalk.

morning

light hangs off the side of
the horizon, reluctant to let go
and fall into the nothing of the nighttime.
it is how i feel when uncertainty hits,
finding myself hanging off the proverbial side,
afraid of falling back into the
                                nothing.

and every morning, the sun and i
rise, skipping child-like over houses
across the sky, nighttime nothing more
than a memory.

sunday

a bird flew by my window,
small breeze formed
by her wings,

       torn from spring.
born in wind blown sighs,

she flies—
balances a word on each

feather tip against the
smooth glass.

so we danced

       to the sound of dishes
       being washed,

and bird calls through an
open window.

grasping

where goes that
elusive desire,
is it lost to fading minutes
thrown about a day?
does she return
to springs of thought
or simply leave me forever,
so that i grasp
to hold her for yet another day?

a quick lesson

there is a place in between
where you begin and where i begin,

and in that place is
ice cream
                in summer.

vanilla spoonfuls
though i know that you prefer the taste
of mint chocolate chip.

so you see, despite myself
and my many
                many
                                shortcomings,
i *can* learn to learn new things.

just another love poem

i write love poems where i say small *nothings*
i think might get the blood
to rise in your face.
speak french where all i know how to say is:
i am the cheese because i am

                           the cheese.
or something more profound…
you see, i am riffing,
trying to impress with my imagery.
and this is just another love poem
where i mention the way you breath
in your sleep, one eye open and
wondering what i'm pulling from
an empty fridge in the middle of the night.
you say you slept fine and dreamt of me doing
the exact same thing.
we'll have this conversation over coffee
that tastes like morning and toothpaste,
in mugs that say things like "just hang in there"
or "brooklyn".
another love poem because i don't know how
else to say that i want nothing else
except to write small *nothings*
and read them to you during commercial breaks
in our underwear
while eating the cheesecake i bought
for just this occasion

destinations

i don't always know where i am
going, only know when i get there.
here i am now
           fat with love,
and frozen rainbows caught
inside the lens of two brown
eyes. we eat sunflower seeds in the grass,
break frail shells between our
teeth to munch on the insides.
delightful, like brass horns in summer,
a concert in the dry heat.
only the odor of creosote bushes
along a low ridge to remind me of the rain,
and those rainbows stamped in my
memory, rushing out like water from a spillway
when the desert heat becomes
too much.

on a muddy road to nowhere

i'm traveling but going nowhere,
holding onto a man i've never met
as he drives us up and down a muddy hill.
we can smell the beach from here,
can hear the waves crashing on an isolated coast
through the rumbling of an old dirt bike.
he asks if i speak spanish—yes i do,
but i can understand it better when
holding a cold *presendente*.
she holds onto me tight as
i struggle with our bags, my arms
wrapped securely around a man i've never met.
we ride towards nowhere and
i know we're getting close because
the sun smacks me in the back like the
hand of the devil;
and when he drops us off all she can do is cry;
"because you're so happy?" i ask.
"no," she says, "because we're alive."
where the beach smells like fried fish,
sun block, and coconut water.
where our guide lopes out of the jungle
with his tail between his legs,
stopping to take a cool piss by the
dried husk of a palm tree, leading us to
warm waters, stopping only to turn back
to make sure we're still following.

on spoons

there is no greater pleasure
than being the
small spoon

        in bed,

with knees tucked
up to my chest and
her arm wrapped around me.

i live my life, most days,
as a ladle
       / a great scooping, metal
       ladle used for soups and
       sauces,

except in those moments
when i am the small spoon.

good for stirring peppermint tea,
or scooping sugar into
black coffee.
blissful within her arms,
making sure that i don't
fall off the bed.

how we dance

we never dance anymore:

like wild flowers growing
            rain
                        falling
honey dripping from
            wooden spoons
            into hot tea

storm clouds brewing
small children spinning
in place

bees with pollen falling
from their dangling legs

no

we dance like old friends
smiling

like wind blown curtains
            or errant blown kisses

            like
                        lovers

or rain in summer &
fresh baked bread
            and willow trees

with nothing to prove
& nowhere to be
and no one else with whom
we'd rather be dancing

how i know she loves me

i often watch her reflection
turn this way and that in a
foggy mirror,

but her visage
            is clear to me.

and when i am lying in bed
on a cold morning,
gripping the woolen blankets with
both hands

she lets me sleep and
whispers, so that i don't wake

"the cat has peed on the bathmat"
            and i know that she loves me.

a short hiatus from daily living

leave the bags on the counter
and take my hand,
the milk can wait the
few minutes it takes to stare
outside the kitchen window

at rain falling on the
swing-set in the back.
the one i fixed last weekend
while you sipped wine
and laughed at the sunset.

and i know you're afraid
of melted ice cream
bleeding onto the counter,
rocky road suffering a slow death
next to the pre-mixed salad

we'll try to eat in time
before the leaves go bad,
but this won't take long, in fact
we're already almost finished.
see, the sun peaking from

behind fat clouds,
feral cats licking the water
from the weeds?
maybe you want to
lean your head on my shoulder,

i'll sweep the hair from your face.
we'll take a long breath
to rest from daily living
like cats on a sunny porch
after a summer rain storm

in the desert where the water

on the ground is already being
called back into the sky.
the ice cream and milk will have
to wait patiently on the counter

while we stand in the kitchen
in love and quiet and feeling
silly that we care about
anything at all outside
 of this moment.

i'm just saying

do you remember the look
on my face when you told
me we were having a baby?
we were on our way to dinner
with my parents,
but that was just a footnote
in the narrative you wrote
with your eyes that night.
we drove in silence knowing
this would be our last drive
as a pair
and as awkward as dinner was,
i have to admit, my mother's
chicken was really good,
despite the maelstrom that
stormed just above the clouds
like much needed rain in the desert.

catching bubbles

i know the futility of catching bubbles
in bare hands,
those blown out of a yellow bubble
blower sitting on the patio table.

but still we try,
and fail, and instead count
our successes not in the number of bubbles
we've caught

but in the minutes spent laughing at the cat
as he tries to catch them too.

and part of my brain is
telling me this is a metaphor
but i can't think for what,

i don't have the time;

we're too busy catching bubbles floating
up between our bouts of laughter

and the cat's fruitless swipes.

how i lacked imagination

we play rock-paper-scissors
and i lose

not because i let him win but
because he's beaten me with
a well placed dinosaur;
hands chomping
          at my fingers.

          at three years old he's decided
          dinosaurs should no doubt
          beat rock paper and/or
          scissors every time

                    which, of course, is true.

when i try to explain that the game
is, in fact not called

rock-paper-scissors-dinosaur,

he shakes his head as if
pitying my lack of imagination
readying himself for
another go.

epilogue

we go out for a late walk,
caught in the post-pumpkin pie
haze of an october evening.
the air tingles the skin,
goose bumps rising in
protest.
we look for bats on the
streetlamps, those made of wood,
the kind that grab at your shirt sleeves
if you veer too close.
her hand sits in mine, fits snugly
like footsteps in the street
on the way to the canal
where joggers let the sound
of city-stained rain water take them
to a far off mountain stream.
and even in the desert,
the trees drop autumn down
on our heads.
a toddler kicks the leaves
into the running waters
so that they float away into
the waning sunset.

While originally born and raised in Brooklyn, NY, **Daniel** currently resides in Phoenix, AZ. He is a poet (and sometimes fiction writer), enjoying the desert lifestyle in lieu of the hustle of the city. He has been fortunate enough to publish the poetry chapbooks *Sunday Morning Ponderings* (Flutter Press, 2015), *Yes I Know You Can't Drive Across The World* (Red Bird Chapbooks, 2016), and *Just Another Love Poem* (Flutter Press, 2017). His work has been featured both online and in print, including in the journals *Westward Quarterly, Poetry Quarterly, Third Wednesday,* and *Avalon Literary Review. How I Learned to Learn New Things* is his debut full-length poetry collection. He has spent time as a poetry editor and a poetry book reviewer. When not writing, Daniel enjoys spending time with his amazing wife and their equally amazing six year old son, both of whom have been incredible influences for his writing. He is currently pursuing an MFA in Creative Writing from Lindenwood University. For news on upcoming publications, visit Daniel's website www.dmosmusings.com. You can follow him on Twitter at @dmos1183.

www.ingramcontent.com/pod-product-compliance
Lightning Source LLC
Chambersburg PA
CBHW070550090426
42735CB00013B/3137